W9-DAD-696

HEROES OF AMERICAN HISTORY

George W. Bush

The 43rd President

Carmen Bredeson

Enslow Publishers, Inc.

40 Industrial Road   PO Box 38
Box 398   Aldershot
Berkeley Heights, NJ 07922   Hants GU12 6BP
USA   UK

http://www.enslow.com

Library of Congress Cataloging-in-Publication Data

Bredeson, Carmen.

   George W. Bush : The 43rd president / Carmen Bredeson.

     v. cm. — (Heroes of American history)

   Includes index.

   Contents: Growing up—Growing family—Election time—President Bush—Tragedy in America.

   ISBN 0-7660-2100-9 (hardcover)

   1. Bush, George W. (George Walker), 1946–   . —Juvenile literature. 2. Presidents—United States—Biography—Juvenile literature. [1. Bush, George W. (George Walker), 1946–   .

2. Presidents.] I.Title. II. Series.

E903 .B74 2002

973.931'092—dc21

                  2002000489

Printed in the United States of America

10 9 8 7 6 5 4 3 2 1

To Our Readers: We have done our best to make sure all Internet Addresses in this book were active and appropriate when we went to press. However, the author and the publisher have no control over and assume no liability for the material available on those Internet sites or on other Web sites they may link to. Any comments or suggestions can be sent by e-mail to comments@enslow.com or to the address on the back cover.

Table of Contents

Baby George grins up at his parents,
George and Barbara Bush.

Chapter 1

Growing Up

People lined the streets, waiting for the parade. Some waved small American flags. As the car carrying the new president and first lady drew closer, cheers filled the air. George and Laura Bush smiled and waved. George W. Bush had just become the forty-third president of the United States.

George Walker Bush was born on July 6, 1946, in New Haven, Connecticut. George's father was a student at Yale University. He was captain of Yale's baseball team. George's mother, Barbara, went to all the games. After baby George was born, she took him along. Maybe this is why her little boy grew up to love baseball.

After George's dad graduated from college in 1948, the family moved to Midland, Texas. Mr. Bush took a job with an oil drilling

Cowboy George rides a real horse.

company. George started first grade at Sam Houston Elementary School.

George played baseball, soccer, and football, but baseball was his favorite. He was a catcher for his Little League team, the Cubs. George's parents took his little sister,

Robin, and his baby brother, Jeb, to see all the games.

Then something terrible happened. When George was seven years old, little Robin became very sick. A few months later she died of leukemia, a kind of cancer.

In the next few years, two more sons, Neil and Marvin, were born to the Bushes. Now George had three brothers to play with. Their backyard in Midland was nice and big. The

Baseball was always George's favorite sport.

children had plenty of room to run with their dogs, Mark and Cosy. School, church, and sports kept everyone busy.

Sometimes the family went to Maine for vacations.

George's grandparents owned a house near the ocean there. The boys enjoyed fishing and boating in the summer.

George attended San Jacinto Junior High School in Midland during seventh grade. He was elected president of his class. Then, in 1959, his family moved to Houston, Texas. Their new house had a big yard with trees to climb, a small field for baseball, and a swimming pool.

Soon after their move, George's mother had a baby girl. She was named Dorothy, and the family nicknamed her Doro.

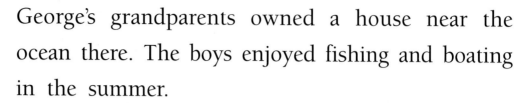

The Bushes in 1956.

Neil

George H.W.

George W.

Barbara

Jeb

Marvin

Little Doro got lots of attention from her four big brothers.

George finished junior high at Kinkaid School in Houston. When it was time for high school, he was sent to Phillips Academy in Andover, Massachusetts. His father had also gone to this all-boys school.

At Phillips Academy, there were many strict rules. Students had to wear jackets and ties to class. They lived in dormitories, where each boy had a bed, a desk, and a closet. They ate breakfast, lunch, and dinner in a big dining room. George was an average student who played on the baseball and basketball teams.

Midland

Dallas

TEXAS

Houston

Austin

9

Chapter 2

College and Career

George started college in 1964. He went to Yale, the same college where his father had gone. George studied history and played baseball and rugby, a kind of football. He liked sports and parties much more than books and studying. He was a popular student who was always ready to have a good time.

When George graduated from Yale in 1968, the United States was fighting in the Vietnam War.

Healthy young men had to serve in the military, and many were sent to fight in Vietnam. George chose to join the Texas Air National Guard. He learned to fly F-102 fighter jets and became a very good pilot. He taught other young men to fly at an Air Force base in Houston, Texas.

George at Yale.

After two years, George became part of the National Guard Reserves. Now he worked for the National Guard part time, instead of full time.

In 1973, when he was twenty-eight years old, George returned to school. He studied business at Harvard University, earning a master's degree in 1975.

What career would George choose? He moved to Midland, Texas, to work in the oil business, just as his dad had done.

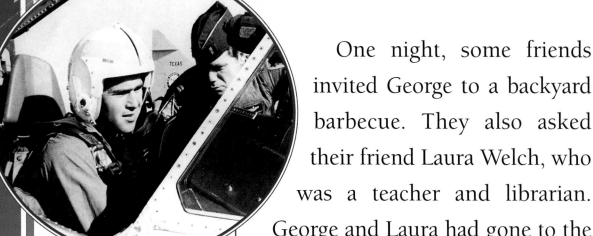

In the Texas Air National Guard, George learned to fly fighter jets.

One night, some friends invited George to a backyard barbecue. They also asked their friend Laura Welch, who was a teacher and librarian. George and Laura had gone to the same junior high school in Midland, but they did not know each other. After meeting Laura, George said, it was "love at first sight." It must have been! George Bush and Laura Welch were married just three months later, on November 5, 1977.

The couple settled into a home in Midland, where George continued to work in the oil business. He was also interested in government and politics. His dad had been a United States congressman from 1966 to 1970. George decided to run for Congress in 1978.

Before the election, George visited many homes

and businesses to talk with the people of Texas. He told them why he would be a good congressman. George and Laura went to meetings and rode in parades. They hoped to win many votes.

But George lost the election. He went back to the oil business.

George's father was having better luck in politics. In 1980, Ronald Reagan was elected president of the United States, and George Herbert Walker Bush was his vice president.

A year later, on November 25, 1981, George and Laura became the parents of twin baby daughters. As the girls grew,

George and Laura on their wedding day.

George and Laura loved to play with them and read books aloud. *Hop on Pop* by Dr. Seuss was a family favorite. While Laura read the book, George would lie on the floor and let the twins hop on him.

When the twins were five years old, their dad made some big changes in his life. He became more serious about his religion and joined a Bible study group. He also gave up drinking. George had always enjoyed going to parties. Sometimes he drank too much. In 1986, at the age of forty, he decided it was time to stop. George still liked to have fun, but he would no longer drink alcohol.

The happy new dad holds his daughters, Jenna and Barbara.

Chapter 3

Election Time

George's dad, George Herbert Walker (H. W.) Bush, was vice president for eight years. Next, he hoped to become president. George W. was eager to help his father win the election. (He is often called George W. so he won't be confused with his dad.)

George W. sold his oil business and moved with Laura and the twins to Washington, D.C. He gave speeches, raised money, and talked to voters about why his father would be a good president. All the hard work was worth it. His dad became president of the United States on January 19, 1989.

The whole Bush family was in Washington to see the new president take the Oath of Office. George's parents moved into the White House.

Barbara and Jenna were seven years old when their grandfather became president. The girls enjoyed running around the White House with their cousins. They also liked bowling in the White House bowling alley.

President George H. W. Bush and First Lady Barbara Bush

Now it was time for George W. and Laura to return to Texas. The oil business had slowed down, so George W. decided to try a different business. That year, he and a group of people bought a major-league baseball team, the Texas Rangers. George, Laura, and the twins moved to Dallas, Texas, to be near the team.

Owning a baseball team was great, but George W. was still thinking about politics. He decided to run for governor of Texas in 1994, when he was forty-eight years old. When George W. won the election, he and Laura packed up the twins and moved to Austin, the state capital.

As governor, Bush worked hard to cut taxes. He also wanted to make education better in the state. Governor Bush believed

George W. and Laura, with Barbara, left, and Jenna.

that every student should be a good reader by the third grade. He knew that students who do not read well have a tough time in school. If they drop out, they cannot get good jobs.

George W. Bush was a very popular Texas governor. In the next election, he was voted in for four more years. People began to ask him if he would like to run for president.

This was a big decision. It would mean many changes for the Bushes. Presidents and their families have very little privacy. How would Laura and the twins feel about this? They would always have Secret Service agents nearby. The agents' job is to protect the president. Also, reporters follow the president and his family everywhere they go. The public likes to know what the president is doing.

George W. talked it over with his family and decided to enter the race for president. For the next year, George and Laura met with people all over America. George explained what he would do to be a good president. He was running against Al Gore, who had been the vice president for eight years under President Bill Clinton.

The election was held on November 7, 2000. Votes were cast, and America waited to see who had won. First, Bush was called the winner. Then it seemed the vote was too close to call. There was a problem with the votes in Florida. They were counted and recounted for weeks. Finally, on December 12, the United States Supreme Court

The 2000 presidential race pitted George Bush against Al Gore, right.

said the counting must stop. The next day, George W. Bush was named the winner of the election.

On January 20, 2001, George W. Bush was sworn in as president of the United States. His whole family was there to watch him take the Oath of Office. It reminded them of the day when his father, George H. W. Bush, had become president in 1989.

George W. and his dad.

The Bush family moved into the White House. Spot and Barney, the dogs, and India the cat settled into their new home. They help keep George and Laura Bush company while the twins are away at college.

Chapter 4

President George W. Bush

President Bush is a very busy man. He gets up early and takes coffee to Laura. After they read the newspapers, it is time for exercise. The president jogs every day and lifts weights to stay strong.

In his office, the real work begins. The president goes to many meetings, talks to senators and congressmen, and signs bills into law. George W. Bush had promised to cut taxes when he became

| George W. Bush | Laura Bush | Barbara Bush | Former President Bill Clinton | Chief Justice William Rehnquist |

President Bush takes the Oath of Office.

president—and he did. A few months after Bush took office, Congress passed a law that cut taxes by $1.35 trillion.

President Bush also convinced Congress to pass a law to improve the nation's schools, just as he had done in Texas. Another of his plans was to drill for oil in wilderness areas of Alaska, but some people in Congress said no. They said it would hurt the environment.

The president also meets with the leaders of many other countries. When the new president of Mexico, Vicente Fox, came to visit, a special dinner was held at the White House. Many important people were invited to meet President Fox.

President Bush likes to stay in shape.

Sometimes President Bush has meetings in other countries. During his first year in office, he visited Japan, China, Korea, El Salvador, Mexico, and Peru. The president travels in his own airplane, which is called Air Force One. This large airliner has a private bedroom, a bathroom with a shower, a meeting room, and plenty of space for the White House staff and reporters.

In the White House, the president

President Bush welcomed Mexican president Vicente Fox, far left, for a visit in 2001.

works in the Oval Office. This room overlooks part of the White House lawn. One day President Bush decided that the lawn would be a great place for a T-ball game.

The president invited the Memphis Red Sox and the Capital City Rockets. Thirty-two children played on the teams, and parents and friends came to cheer. The game was followed by a picnic on the White House lawn.

Chapter 5

Tragedy in America

During the summer of 2001, President and Mrs. Bush spent the month of August at their Texas ranch. Then they returned to Washington, all rested and ready to get back to work.

On September 11, 2001, a terrible thing happened in America. Two airplanes slammed into the World Trade Center buildings in New York City. Another plowed into the Pentagon in Washington, D.C.,

President Bush visited New York City after the attack on the World Trade Center.

while a fourth plane crashed in Pennsylvania. Terrorists had hijacked all four planes. America was under attack.

President Bush was visiting with schoolchildren in Florida when he got the news. The Secret Service rushed him to Air Force One. By the time his plane was in the air, both World Trade Center buildings had crashed to the ground. Thousands of innocent people were trapped inside and died. Rescue crews dug through the rubble, looking for survivors.

People all over the United States cried and waved American flags. President Bush said that the terrorists were trying to tear America apart. "But they have failed," he said. "Our country is strong." He promised to work hard to track down the people who caused the attacks. He asked other world leaders to join together to fight against terrorism.

While the war on terrorism is going on, the president also has other work to do. He must make sure the economy stays strong. Are there enough jobs for everyone? Can all Americans afford to buy the things that they need? What can the government do to help people?

The president believes that all children should be able to live happy lives. In January 2002, he signed a new law. This law gives more money to help children who need to be adopted or who need foster families. He hopes that every child who needs a loving family will find one.

George Walker Bush became president at a difficult time for the

United States. But presidents are elected to guide the country through good times and bad. Great presidents do that well, and more than anything, George W. Bush wants to be a great president.

George W. Bush faces many challenges as president of the United States.

Timeline

1946~George Walker Bush is born on July 6.

1964~Graduates from Phillips Academy in Massachusetts.

1968~Graduates from Yale University with a degree in history.

1969~Joins the Texas Air National Guard.

1975~Earns a master's degree in business from Harvard University.

1977~Marries Laura Welch on November 5.

1981~Twin girls, Barbara and Jenna, are born.

1988~His father, George H. W. Bush, is elected forty-first president of the United States.

1994~George W. is elected governor of Texas.

1998~Elected to a second term as governor.

2000~Elected forty-third president of the United States.

Words to Know

congressman—A lawmaker in the government.

economy—The way the money and goods of a country are managed.

hijack—To take control of a vehicle by force.

master's degree—An advanced course of study for people who have finished college.

National Guard—A force of soldiers who protect the United States.

Oath of Office—A promise to do a good job.

politics—The workings of government.

terrorist—Someone who causes great fear, usually through violence.

Learn More

Books

Aaseng, Nathan. *The White House*. San Diego, Calif.: Lucent Books, 2001.

St. George, Judith. *So You Want to Be President*. New York: Philomel Books, 2000.

Wade, Mary Dodson. *George W. Bush: Governor of Texas*. Austin, Tex.: W. S. Benson, 1999.

Internet Addresses

The White House for Kids
  <http://www.whitehouse.gov/kids/>

George W. Bush
  <http://www.georgebush.com>

Index

JB
Bush

Bredeson, Carmen
George W. Bush